M000005987

On the Mezzanine

Cassie Donish

Copyright © 2019 by Cassie Donish
All rights reserved

Cover art by Todd Thomas Brown, "Being Without Ground," 2018
Book design by Natalie Eilbert
Published by Gold Line Press
http://goldlinepress.com
Gold Line titles are distributed through Small Press Distribution.
This title is also available for purchase directly from the publisher.
www.spdbooks.org : 800.869.7553

Library of Congress Cataloging-in-Progress Data
On the Mezzanine : Cassie Donish
Library of Congress Control Number 2015942420
Donish, Cassie
978-1-938900-28-0

On the Mezzanine

I also am other than what I imagine myself to be. To know this is forgiveness.

—SIMONE WEIL

Where is there a room
without the damn god of love?

—MICHAEL ONDAATJE

The confession reaches through and beyond its obvious quest for forgiveness or absolution. It is directed toward another kind of psychological gain. It seeks ultimately to overcome time.

—LYN HEJINIAN

℞

One year, I imagined life as a series of opening and closing elevator doors, and nearby, a series of moving walkways on which some figures are standing, some walking, some running. There are escalators too, and stairwells, and large screens on which flash images of these same mechanisms of movement. A set of doors opens, and there is one's mother, father, sister, brother, daughter, son; there is one's lover, one's friend; the doors close again, a fragment of a greeting hanging in the air, or an entire lifetime of conversation, echoes punctuating the stillness, like the feeling of a room just after a lover has gone.

~

That year, in between seasons, as winter turned to spring, I watched (this is *now*; I am watching) as doors opened and closed. In the park, the pavilions stood ceremoniously. The towering trees were bare, except for the matching junipers, whose needles, when rubbed between fingers, left the smell of gin even in the coldest week. Each day new color tore through vision, shades elicited by the internal, singular clocks each organic thing seems to harbor. Yellow flare of forsythia, here, here, now there too; Japanese magnolias, their pink and purple teacups, their exquisite lean.

3

~

Yes, the year I speak of is *now*—just into spring, nearly April, month of cruel pleasures. Human social life is a continuous flow of offerings and requests; each sound you and I uttered, a form of, "Can you, will you, accept this?"

Of all the moments, where to begin? We sat at the table in my living room. On the phone earlier that day, you'd said, "You're avoiding me."

"Yes, I am. Doesn't that make sense in our situation?" I'd said.

You showed up at my apartment anyway.

Something red tore through the room.

~

"Where are 'things'? In amorous space, or in mundane space?" asks Roland Barthes.

I realize I've been wondering about this for a long time.

On the kitchen counter, an open bottle of tequila, a skeleton on its label; in the bathroom, various shades of eye shadow, and makeup brushes strewn; on the windowsill, your phone playing music; on the bed, the sheets not yet torn.

4

~

We'd each left a person standing in a room, we'd entered a new room through opposite facing doors of sliding glass. Now we were together, standing, embraced. Over my shoulder, you could see the person I'd left through the glass. Over yours, I could see the person you'd left. Beside her, there was a child. From the looks on their faces, I could tell they couldn't see me.

~

The first time I put makeup on you, straddling your lap. After which we made love for the first time, and violently. Black eyeliner, a smear of shimmering eye shadow the color of tea with milk, black mascara. Some lipstick. "I'm putting the exact makeup on you that I have on," I said. It was what I had with me. You said you felt *seen*. This was one of those weeks where I can still recall everything: your look in the café on Thursday, the text on Friday, the Saturday storm, and now it was Sunday. "Tell me if I go too far, okay?" you whispered gently above me.

~

I wonder when you began to turn irrevocably in my direction. One day, six months earlier, we talked for hours, moved between bars, skipped our other engagements to continue what you later called our "seminal conversation."

C, I saw something in you, a mystery shade glowing through a tightly gridded screen, a green exterior. I asked about it. You didn't falter.

To use another metaphor: it seems my comments revealed wide spaces in the jigsaw puzzle of your life, showing that it had been put together wrong. That it was going to be disassembled.

~

Between inhale and exhale—the pause at the crest. Liminal space between seasons. That passing stillness.

Moments of confusion in trying to find a word for an indeterminate color. The freedom and paralysis of namelessness. This is where we are, this is where we've languished.

The concept of liminality was developed by anthropologists to describe the ambiguity that occurs during the middle stage of rituals of initiation.

Say you're the initiant, and you're entering the ritual circle to move from the category of "boy" to the category of "man" (or, let's imagine, from "masculine" to "feminine"; or vice versa; or other crossings we're approaching, whether or not we know it yet). When you step into the circle, you are temporarily outside both categories. For the duration of the ritual, inside that space, you transcend your culture and society; since you exist in neither category, you are nameless, and therefore close to the divine. When you exit the circle, you have transformed.

You have crossed into a new category. You have a new name.

~

Say we stood on a moving walkway. There were others around us: colleagues, cashiers, artists, neighbors, police officers, grad students, family members, protesters, strangers. There were also streetlights, trees, shopping districts, and all the reflective mirrors that make up a city. All at once—it's difficult to pinpoint the moment, I am trying, I will try—a trapdoor.

"Yes," says a woman I'll call Elias. "It's as though you fell through a trapdoor." Friends seemed to speak to me from behind a curtain. They became a chorus of faceless individuals, unable to penetrate the scene; I called all of them by the same name.

From the moving walkway, you and I fell into my living room (amorous space). Where the only movement was circular, organic. We breathed into each other's mouths until we were dizzy.

Barthes: "I suddenly see myself caught in the trap, immobilized in an impossible situation (site): there are only two ways out (either…or) and they are both barred: nothing to be said in either direction."

It was clear we should leave immediately, or stay indefinitely; these the only options, and neither felt possible.

"Desire is a moment with no way out," writes Anne Carson.

~

A mutual acquaintance—another Elias, say—had mentioned each of our names to the other. One of us got ahold of the other's email address, and after a few exchanges, we'd met. Our rapport was immediate; not flirtatious, but exceedingly warm.

You were energetic. Highly productive. (*Unusually* energetic, *unusually* productive, we'd understand later.) We were both writers. You had studied historiography (time); I had studied geography (space). For some reason, this made us laugh. We discussed working on a collaborative project.

Something about my nature, it seems now, was always going to unearth something in yours. I asked the right questions without knowing it, was attentive in the right ways.

Perhaps it was because your secrets were exactly my obsessions. Something about your nature was going to unearth something in me too, though it took me longer to understand this. I still don't understand it, but I'm trying to begin (but where to begin?).

~

You're subletting a room in a house you never go to. We keep my

8

green curtains closed. I have a neighbor who knows the woman who is still your wife. I worry about how insular our experience has been. Our involvement, hidden. Our music, constant.

"What if you're just trading one secret for another?" I ask. You confessed to your encounters just after the vernal equinox. Among other things, you told them (your wife, your pastor) you'd lost your faith. Your spiritual orientation, also queered.

"I don't want anyone to think this is happening because of you," you say. "You may have been a catalyst, but you're not the cause. I want people in my life to be open to knowing you. And right now, they won't be."

When we're in public, you don't hold my hand. You don't smile or hold my gaze. Some days I'm filled with repetitive, fearful thoughts. These are my own (who else's?).

"And it is tempting to touch each other inappropriately / In order to pretend that all is fine with the world"—Maged Zaher

~

At some point, years before meeting you, I'd underlined the following two sentences in Michael Ondaatje's memoir, *Running in the Family*: "It seems that most of my relatives at some time were attracted to somebody they shouldn't have been. Love affairs rainbowed over

9

marriages and lasted forever—so it often seemed that marriage was the greater infidelity." There was a danger always present in me, in my body, a danger only barely recognized as danger and only distantly, intellectually, the danger of a secret, of desire that occurs in the stairwell just outside the party, when you are drunk on wine or whiskey, in a city not your own.

~

The walls of my apartment become mobile, animate; they are dynamic, expanding and contracting. Here we begin your ritual.

"Man only escapes from the laws of this world in lightning flashes. Instants when everything stands still, instants of contemplation, of pure intuition, of mental void, of acceptance of the moral void," writes Simone Weil.

From now on I won't call myself *mistress*, I won't call myself *lover*. I will call myself *officiant*. But since I have no official training, I admit I'm concerned.

~

On the phone, a dear friend—I call him Elias also—used a phrase that stayed with me, although it sounded lofty at first. He spoke of the necessity of "adjusting one's narrative toward reality." He was very ill at the time; perhaps he wouldn't recover. The sound of his voice reminded me of cities he and I had been in together, the bodies of water we'd sat beside. The sound of his voice contained the voices of others, events already written and ones not yet written, the sound of his wife's love.

You and I then discussed the phrase "adjusting our narrative toward reality." How important it was to do this, to practice acceptance. (But we left out the question of reality itself. The question of *what is*.)

~

What's real: rose orange glow, the streetlamp outside the window. That pink light on your face. Salt of your skin on my tongue. The mattress on the floor. You're breathing hard above me, threshing. When I ask you to hurt me, it's not about pain, exactly. I want you to take me to the edge of the canyon. I beg. Don't let go of my hand. I'm burning in the sun.

~

Two nights ago, I said to you in bed, "Being with you like this is almost unbearable."

(I almost said "unbearably beautiful.")

Your eyes were wide. Your lips, parted as if you were trying to speak. Finally you said, "I want to talk, but I don't have language."

I said, "I know."

We were barely touching. I watched your pupils dilate at the slightest sensation.

My hands will never leave your shoulders. They will never leave your collarbone.

You said, "I'm dying," just as I was thinking it. *I'm dying.*

At its root perhaps my anxiety comes from living in a culture that knows more about violence than sensuality. I would rather practice the latter, I would rather take the latter too far, I would rather die from the latter.

~

Oberyn Martell, a prince of Dorne in *Game of Thrones*, is beautiful, bisexual, and a legendary fighter. He shows up in King's Landing with Ellaria Sand, his sensuous, bisexual, fierce lover. The two go to a brothel; they find a pretty young woman for her, a gorgeous young man for him, and they playfully mess around, all on one bed.

I watch with too much interest. I am an opportunistic viewer of the scene. I'm trying to externalize my experience with you, my experience of you. Maybe it's this: I'm looking for representations of us.

"You like them both the same, boys and girls?" the young man says to Oberyn.

"Does that surprise you?"

"Everyone has a preference."

"Then everyone is missing half the world's pleasure. The gods made that," Oberyn says, nodding to the naked young woman, "and it delights me. The gods made this," he says, and smacks the young man's ass, "and it delights me."

Ellaria crawls toward Oberyn, climbs on top of him, says lustily, "He is a prince of Dorne. Girls and boys will line up to fuck him till the day he dies."

"They will all have to line up behind you," Oberyn says as she straddles him.

~

On some days, you think about dying—not from sensuality but from grief. You retreat into yourself beside me. You feel the softness of your own skin with a different kind of desire. Scars, on your ankle. Your eyes become intense, distant. You ask me to hide sharp objects from you. Often, it's after an exchange with your wife, from whom you are now separated. After the two of you talk about your son. You lie with your head in my lap. You touch your sternum. You're short of breath. "I can't—" you say.

I can't actually be writing any of this.

I understand deception, though not at the level you practiced it. I know to use the word "practice" isn't quite correct. It implies a certain degree of intentionality I don't believe you had, even as you led a double life, impulsively meeting up with men for years, using an alias, never telling any of them your real name.

~

The small things, and how I want to gather them to me. Leaves the color of blood, covering my childhood street every fall, and the girl in high school who used to suck my nipples for hours in one of our beds, or behind the low cement wall of an apartment garden.

How long it took this year to get to spring.

I remember that day at the very end of winter—there were some red blossoms already on the trees—when we walked west through the park, and then back. We paused to face each other under a pavilion. We didn't hold each other yet. Each phrase (each blossom) intimated a spring we would spend together. Such things can be said in hindsight. The memory is a photograph (you and I, walking under trees). The memory is a beautiful ghost. Something floated by us, and we held it.

Barthes: "From the start, greedy to play a role, scenes take their position in memory: often I feel this, I foresee this, at the very moment when these scenes are forming."

~

There is always a lot of green in my memory of that day. I want it to overtake me.

I also remember your eyes, the way you looked at me the first time we met. The air around you shone brighter, moved faster. We sat at a small table in a café across from the university.

It is unfortunate how much I remember.

Weil writes, "We must prefer real hell over imaginary paradise." She writes of the renunciation of past and future (they are imaginary).

I've been disturbed lately by the word "adore." I remember the way my mother used it when I was a child, the way she talked about men she loved. I found it beautiful at the time.

Now I'm scared to think the word.

~

While the young woman is going down on her, Ellaria reaches over to the young man, who's kissing Oberyn. She pulls the young man's face to hers, kisses him. "You're greedy," Oberyn teases.

After kissing him for a moment more, she says to the young man, "No?"

"I'm sorry," he says. "You're lovely, I just never acquired the taste."

"You're calling my beauty an acquired taste?" says Oberyn.

"That's quite all right, lover," says Ellaria. "More for you."

The absolute trust between them, the love, the camaraderie and playfulness, the pleasure taken in each other's pleasure—even pleasure in others, other lovers, other bodies—isn't this what we felt? The fact of being with others would not (will not) matter. We were going to be this couple; and it would be, against all odds, eventually, perfect.

Carson: "The difference between what is and what could be is visible. The ideal is projected on a screen of the actual, in a kind of stereoscopy."

~

The fan's blades spin so fast I can't see them. The cycle of days becomes a blur—the windows, open; the light of an afternoon storm floods in; you sit at my table, a current of electricity running across the room between our bodies. A new lover is real, and symbolizes the real. I turn and think of saying, "The white sky today glows through a density of green, this contrast feels expansive"; you'd say, "My pain hasn't affected my enjoyment of our days."

The first sign of the turn would be if one of us said, "It hasn't *yet*."

At the beginning, we promised not to make each other promises. It was the first promise we would break. And we would break it the hardest, it would be obliterated, atomized.

Barthes: "In amorous panic, I am afraid of my own destruction, which I suddenly glimpse, inevitable, clearly formed." I admit I was already afraid at the beginning.

~

Back, before.

The first time you mentioned where you grew up, we were at a rooftop bar after a reading, gin and tonics in hand. It was winter. My jacket was still on, and my hand was cold, wet with condensation from my glass. You mumbled. The name of the country narrowly escaped your mouth.

"Why don't I know this about you?" I said. We had talked about places we'd each lived before, but you'd never mentioned this.

"I guess I don't really offer details about my past unless I'm asked a specific question," you said.

I was tipsy. "So I should've asked if you'd grown up there, specifically?" I said. "You compartmentalize your life." You looked hurt, and I felt awful. "That came out harshly. I don't know why I said that. I shouldn't have said it that way. I'm sorry."

"Hey, no—it's okay," you said. Your voice sounded sad, and there was a sudden unexpected tenderness between us. At the time, you were still my married Christian friend with a son.

Each successive time you've talked about your encounters with men, you've implied that they happened with greater frequency.

~

I want to take you to the park, and in order to convince you to come with me, I begin to describe it to you. But I only describe the pretty things. There's so much I don't want to look at, don't want to notice, and when I realize this I begin to panic. That's why I begin to mention the trash, the smoke, burnt bits of paper, empty cigarette packs, crushed soda cans on the path. But I also insist on calling these beautiful. Cement blocks. Dogshit in the grass. A dead bird, splayed. I can't help it.

The dog walkers are glamorous. And the golden bells of flowers. Their lovely finish. It may be my mood. Months go by. When I touch you, you say, "Your hands rearrange me."

I want to call everything beautiful. You, asleep on my couch, devastated. I wonder if the desire to call everything beautiful implicates me, my ease of position, my power. I want to say how one thing has led to another. In some moments, I do believe in cause.

I want to write you into my story, yet I can barely write, and today you can barely speak. I want to obviate the theme of us through its rendering. I want to write about my love for you and thereby destroy it. I mean this to be affirming. I don't mean destruction, I mean proliferation.

~

You knew much more about me. That my parents and older sisters were in a cult for more than a decade before I was born. That my two sisters and I have three different fathers. That I have another sister on my dad's side, with a different mother. That I had struggled with monogamy, with romantic partnerships. That I could often pass for straight, even though I wasn't.

That I too had hidden things from partners. A stolen moment against a brick wall in an alley, or a walk at night beside a river with a friend, intoxicated, arm-in-arm—the recognition, the turn toward each other that always feels somehow unexpected (this is partly naivety).

~

Sometimes I want to slow things down between us, I try. "The way we talk, it scares me."

You hold my shoulders: "Don't you feel it? Don't you feel how amazing we are together?"

"You're just starting to become who you are," I say. "How can you know what you want right now?"

You're emphatic: "Listen. I do know what I want, and it's you. Don't you want me too?"

I'm crying, because I do. You hold me tightly, your whole body vibrates, you seem like you're about to burst.

~

Your psychiatrist will say later that you've been "running hot" for a long time. We'll learn other ways of describing your high energy, your body's vibrating. *Elevated (euphoric) mood. Flight of ideas. Inflated self-esteem. Increase in goal-directed activity.*

Each day, I hold you. After each coming-out conversation, through the migraines, the text fights with your wife, the way you fall apart after visits with your three-year-old son. At night, we fuck.

"These days with you have been some of the best days of my life," you say.

I slide a slice of peach with mint into your mouth. I remind you that these have also been some of the worst days of your life.

~

You grew up in another country, in various rural areas, the child of missionaries. You were the second eldest of six children, three boys and three girls. Your father told you and your siblings to never marry someone whose parents were divorced. No one in your family has ever been divorced, going back generations.

My parents were divorced, my mom's parents were divorced, and my mom's mom's parents were divorced. And my great-grandmother never knew her father, who had never married her mother.

~

When a friend, another Elias, visited me last year, he read one of my poems and said, "The woman's love might need to have an object again." His pale eyes flickered as I drove him through the park.

It was just before this story began.

He seemed wholesome, yet I decided to trust him with the dark gems of my shame, which I'd been polishing each day before placing them back in their protective case.

I mean I would trust him with my story, its future, my outcome.

(I almost said, "she would trust him with her story, its future…" I almost slipped into the third person; that would have been a mistake.)

~

I admit that sex has always seemed to me inextricably tied not only to mortality, but also to immortality. Not only to the physical, but to the metaphysical. That's not exactly what I mean. I want to say *spirituality*, but I've been soured on the word for years. Though I still use it pragmatically in conversation.

"It's sex, and it isn't— / whatever."—Carl Phillips

"We were made fools of."—Louise Glück

How separate can I be from the world? From my own body, my sex, my gender? We wake up and look at each other's bodies with immediate hunger. We race to whisper words of admiration. Your smell transforms the morning into something animate; the morning becomes the knowing subject; it objectifies us, it renders us, it does with us what it will.

~

My maternal grandmother, who died before I was born, slept with my mom's first lover. "Before, during, and after the time I was sleeping with him," I've heard my mom say more than once. She was seventeen at the time. When she and my aunt found out—a box of letters, given to them by their mother's best friend—their mother had been dead for almost two decades. "I waited until you two were adults, but I think it's important for people to know who their parents really are."

I was in my teens when my mom read the letters. The lists of men. And one in particular that stood out, that made her heart pound in her ears, that made her body go numb.

~

I'm inside our sex, looking out of it into a world of sentences, thoughts, words, symbols it has generated, it has *been*. I'm looking out of it into more language, texts I'm reading and the one I'm writing.

"Does the text have a human form, is it a figure, an anagram of the body? Yes, but of our erotic body. The pleasure of the text is irreducible to physiological need."

If Barthes compared reading and writing to the erotic, I can only compare our erotic life to the pleasure of language. And so I invert his question: is my body an anagram of some kind of text? Yes, if the text is erotic, alive.

~

I want to hold on to every moment I've had with you, every smile and expression, every word, every touch, every part of your body, every kiss, every scent, every hour. Your skin has the warm glow of an apricot. When we make love, I lick you everywhere, I pull your hair, I pull your face toward mine. I can't stand not seeing your eyes. "Look at me," I say, "look at me right now," and they open, two slits from which light pours; they open, two windows through which I can see a dark blue universe, stippled with clouds of water or stars. I can see love.

I see that it is irradiant.

~

She can see a dark blue universe, stippled with clouds of water or stars; she can see love. Sometimes she does slip into the third person. This happens when she feels distant from a sense of agency, when she feels she is outside her own story, watching. This is something dark and familiar. Something ancestral is being skirted by these days, these protracted mornings and evenings she spends with her lover. Long ago, there were tall figures moving around her, each surrounded by their own private darknesses in the rooms and hallways of her childhood home: the father who left and who is now dead, the older sisters, the mother (whose darkness looked like light); and also, the other father. Each of them carried inside a solid and impeccable weight, each was different, and each she watched, learning to pay close attention to the way the heaviness shifted or didn't shift. In this way she must have learned to move in response to another.

~

After my dad left my mom, she had a new partner. She and I moved into his small apartment. The three of us lived in that apartment for the next ten years, until I moved out and went to college. I called him my stepdad when I talked about him, although they were never married. Less than two years after I moved out, they broke up.

He had children of his own, two sons with different mothers. One son was older, around the age of my sisters. The other was younger than me and didn't know that my stepdad was his father; he only knew him as a friend of his mother's. She was married, and she threatened to disappear if my stepdad ever tried to claim legal rights to his son.

It turned out that my stepdad also had an older daughter who everyone had thought was his niece. He'd slept with his brother's wife.

~

I need Weil because I need to learn how to love differently, and better. I need to give up illusions in order to hold on to love. I think it was a friend named Elias who said that in order to love the world (real hell), you must give up everything else (imaginary paradise).

~

But first I want to talk about sensuality as primary, not as a means to an end, not as a path toward sex or sexuality—or even eroticism—though it may and often does lead to those. I want to talk about sensuality as both expressive of and productive of intimacy, but it's more than that. (Weil writes, "Every act should be considered from the point of view not of its object but of its impulsion. The question is not 'What is the aim?' It is 'What is the origin?'")

~

The morning after the first time we had sex, we almost went to see *The Danish Girl,* a movie based on the life of Lili Elbe, a Danish trans woman and one of the earliest known recipients of gender confirmation surgery.

More accurately, the movie is based on a historical novel called *The Danish Girl*, a fictionalized account of Einar Wegener/Lili Elbe's life and her relationship with Gerda (Gottlieb) Wegener, who married Lili before her transition, when she was still known as Einar.

We don't remember now why we were talking about seeing the movie. We're both sure I'm the one who brought it up. Perhaps it's because I put makeup on you, kissed you deeply, rubbed your chest and shoulders hard, ran my fingers through your hair and pulled it gently. You looked unbelievably beautiful and sad; for the first time, your eyes seemed completely open to me.

I pushed my body against you as if trying to enter you. Until, finally—because I didn't yet know what more to do with this particular desire—you took over.

~

According to your family's Christianity, your wife's Christianity, having queer desires is not wrong, but acting on those desires is unequivocally wrong.

Turning away from God is the worst thing that can happen to a person. Also, divorce.

~

"I've been getting strange urges on the road," you told me, hesitant. On the hardest days—another email from your wife, another exchange about your son—you'd start imagining crashing the car into the wall of a building. You decided to stop driving.

I didn't know how real the danger had become until later, when we sat together in your psychiatrist's office. "I knew I shouldn't drive for a while the day I took my hands off the wheel and accelerated until I had drifted over two lanes." You sounded so articulate, your tone was so controlled, it was difficult to hear what you were saying.

~

Once I moved toward a lake with such slowness that my movement was nearly imperceptible. I wanted the lake, but also, I experienced it through distance. I wanted it, or I wanted its blue-green color, its texture—sensuality doesn't ask the difference between a thing and its attributes. In this way sensuality has its own intelligence.

Sensuality has no language; it does not differentiate; it does not name. It does not rely on outcomes; it makes no investments; it is the promise of itself; it is the promise of blue-green, it is the dream of immersion in water.

It is also the dream of trust. (I already had the lake, through apprehending it.)

~

In the early months of our friendship—before I knew anything—I recommended the show *Transparent* to you. I was interested in the show's explorations of gender and sexuality, and its Jewish characters reminded me of my dad, of my family.

You watched the first episode. It freaked you out. You didn't watch any more.

"Are you saying that you're going to start dressing up like a lady all the time?" Sara, the eldest of the three adult siblings in the show, asks her father early in the first season.

"No, honey. All my life, my whole life I've been dressing up—like a man." Maura takes her daughter's hand and presses it against her heart. "This is me."

~

I watch and invest in these narratives—Lili Elbe played by Eddie Redmayne, Maura Pfefferman played by Jeffrey Tambor—while simultaneously being disturbed at seeing cis-men play the parts of trans women. And disturbed at their subsequent critical acclaim, their garnering of various accolades—nominations, awards, etc.—for their portrayals.

Carol Grant, a trans woman, writes: "It's discomforting as hell being so early in my own transition and seeing words like 'bravery' and 'heroism' used to describe Redmayne, even though he'll be able to shed off the experience after his probable Oscar win, all the while having it be a matter-of-fact point of life for me and millions other trans women like me."

(Redmayne was nominated, but didn't win the Oscar.)

~

But I also must admit that the character I've become obsessed with in *The Danish Girl* is perhaps not Lili, but Gerda, played by Alicia Vikander. Her performance is irreproachable; even articles that critique the film's casting and other choices of representation often commend her portrayal. Her large brown eyes swell with tears. Her eyes are reflective mirrors in which we see Lili's confusion, Lili's hurt.

The movie doesn't address the question of Gerda's sexuality, the possibility that she was bisexual or a lesbian. Here, I don't use the word "queer" only because it's not a word that would've been used at the time. But what I mean, in my time, is that the movie doesn't deal with the question of Gerda's queerness.

~

When you were a teenager and got your ear pierced, your conservative, religious mother told you that you looked gay, a plaintive tone in her voice. By this time, you knew you were attracted to men; coming out was nowhere near a possibility you could imagine. When I was eleven, I told my mom about having feelings for a girl I knew in school. We were having lunch at a Thai restaurant. I was confused. I cried. My mom barely blinked and said she thought it was natural.

~

On a bus, reading James Baldwin's novel, *Giovanni's Room*, this is the passage that makes me cry, sitting next to a stranger: "For I

34

am—or I was—one of those people who pride themselves on their willpower…People who believe that they are strong-willed and the masters of their destiny can only continue to believe this by becoming specialists in self-deception."

I remembered the early months of our friendship, when I would occasionally think to myself, "Who *is* this person?"

In addition to being a scholar and a writer, you were a husband, a father, an athlete, a recreational musician and visual artist; you always had multiple projects on the side of your main endeavors, and you were consistently making progress on all of them. You were incredibly busy, disciplined. You once described your daily routine to me (somewhat boastfully), and I wondered if you had any room to breathe; but then, lacking information, I shrugged to myself, and my thoughts moved on.

~

Baldwin's narrator continues: "Their decisions are not really decisions at all—a real decision makes one humble, one knows that it is at the mercy of more things than can be named—but elaborate systems of evasion, of illusion…I had decided to allow no room in the universe for something which shamed and frightened me. I succeeded very well—by not looking at the universe, by not looking at myself, by remaining, in effect, in constant motion. Even constant motion, of course, does not prevent an occasional mysterious drag, a drop, like an airplane hitting an air pocket. And there were a number of those…all sordid…"

I saw that this was exactly how you had been living: in constant motion, with everything regimented, so that you would never have to stop, to look at who you were, to look at what you were doing when no one you knew was watching.

~

The specter of my biological grandmother has haunted me. When I think of the fact that she slept with my mother's first lover, of how my mother suffered this betrayal unknowingly, I feel a retroactive helplessness. My chest tightens. This secret changed the course of my mother's life. When she was in her late teens, still in high school, she left home. My grandmother had called her a bad daughter and kicked her out of the house. My mother then joined a cult, which she would be in for the next fifteen years. She met the fathers of her three daughters; each of these men would eventually leave her.

Sometimes I think that my sisters and I were born with broken hearts, because my mother's heart was already broken before we were born, broken by the woman who bore her (though I also feel this thinking is unfair, deterministic). Maybe our grandmother's heart was broken too. There's a story about how when she was a child, while her mother was braiding her hair, she would glare hatefully at her father. No one knew why.

~

In *Giovanni's Room*, Baldwin writes a white American man living in France who, through his affair with an Italian man named Giovanni, is confronted with his attraction to men. While this narrator, David, does not explicitly address or seem to consider his own whiteness, critics have written about how the book reflects American race relations through the way Baldwin writes the dynamics between characters of different nationalities—American, French, Italian. Others have discussed how David is convincing precisely because he, being white, doesn't think about race, showing the obliviousness of white people to their own racial experience.

In an interview, Baldwin said, "I certainly could not possibly have—not at that point in my life—handled the other great weight, the 'Negro problem.' The sexual-moral light was a hard thing to deal with. I could not handle both propositions in the same book."

~

And yet, while many critics have talked about the book as an exploration of the theme of same-sex desire, Baldwin says in another interview that his book was "not so much about homosexuality, it is what happens if you are so afraid that you finally cannot love anybody."

~

Those weeks of late spring. We'd lie on my couch facing each other, we'd talk for hours, your eyes alight with thought, one of your hands always under my shirt, your thumb moving over my nipple, keeping me in a state of constant arousal.

Carson: "The moment when the soul parts on itself in desire is conceived as a dilemma of body and senses. On Sappho's tongue, as we have seen, it is a moment bitter and sweet."

Can't you slit me open along my prime meridian, can't I slit you open? Can't we press ourselves together, suture our edges?

~

Anxiety is made of circles. I want you, I don't want to lose you, I could lose you, what if I lose you, what if I'm wrong (what if I lose you).

Weil writes, "A great many people do not feel with their whole soul that there is all the difference in the world between the destruction of a town and their own irremediable exile from that town." I read this sentence over and over thinking of your body.

She writes, "Attachment is no more nor less than an insufficiency in our sense of reality. We are attached to the possession of a thing because we think that if we cease to possess it, it will cease to exist."

If I believe that what we have is real, I can let go of my anxieties about what might happen. And I do believe that what we have is real—that it exists. (Don't I?)

~

Perhaps this is also why I depend so much on poetry, which, Lyn Hejinian writes, "comes to know *that* things are. But this is not knowledge in the strictest sense; it is, rather, acknowledgement—and that constitutes a sort of unknowing. To know *that* things are is not to know *what* they are, and to know *that* without *what* is to know otherness (i.e., the unknown and perhaps unknowable)."

I don't know *what* this experience with you is; I know *that* it is, that its reality for both of us, through these last months, has been extraordinarily real; not exceptional, but rather as if many other things that came before were exceptions. (Exceptions to reality.)

~

Sometimes I tighten, struck with rage and fear.

"Maybe arrogance, pride, and shame are the same thing," I said to you a few nights ago.

When you came out as queer to your father recently, he said he knew there was *something*, but he didn't know what it was. He said when you were young you had a sharp streak of prideful anger that seemed without a source.

"To love a stranger as oneself implies the reverse: to love oneself as a stranger," writes Weil.

~

Barthes: "So I accede, fitfully, to a language without adjectives. I love the other, not according to his (accountable) qualities, but according to his existence…I love, not what he is, but *that* he is."

~

Simmering leaves now, leaves sweating. Time passes, and as it passes, you speak of time, you speak of temporal scale. The experience of an hour, you say, doesn't inform our perception of days; days don't inform weeks, weeks don't inform months, years, centuries. Lévi-Strauss: "It is no more possible to pass between the dates which compose the different domains than it is to do so between natural and irrational numbers."

In a city in another state, a man shoots up a gay nightclub that's hosting a Latin night. It all happens in three hours, between two o'clock and five o'clock in the morning. He kills forty-nine people and wounds fifty-three more before being killed by police.

The man was reported to have frequented the nightclub.

The news is always on, even when it's not. The buzz of it in my head. Other mass shootings, often with a white male shooter. An election year, a frightening candidate who everyone I know believes will lose. Every day, the killing of women at the hands of intimate partners. Black men killed by police. The disproportionate killing of black trans women. Bathroom laws. Same-sex marriage. "Equal protection."

Sometimes we feel unsafe, but other times, often times, our privilege protects us. We're straight-passing white queers, though lately, we seem to be passing less. We both grew up poor, but we have cultural capital because of our whiteness, our education. Our relative safety implicates us. The room we're in, my apartment, the block, the neighborhood, the city, the state, the nation—geographies of scale, how they seem to dissolve. None of these domains exist on their own. The rooms we're in, our bodies, shot through with connections to the world outside these walls.

The conditions that make our story possible are the looming backdrop of every scene in which we speak, touch, kiss; but if you turn the scene around, the conditions are in the foreground, and we appear behind them as fragments, ephemeral, illustrative, disappearing.

~

Green June, early summer. We stay up later and later, sing louder, fuck harder. You eat less, bike more, barely sweat.

I don't know if this story will ever know fall, or winter.

"Language is nothing but meanings, and meanings are nothing but a flow of contexts," writes Hejinian. The same must be true of our identities, their relationality. We don't exist in isolation—even though existence, at times, can feel so isolating.

If something can be said, it can be said of anything. We wake up in a room that could have been anyone's, in bodies that could've been anyone's. But for today they're ours; and yours is mine, and mine is yours.

Ani l'dodi v'Dodi li. I am my beloved's and my beloved is mine.

CB

One evening, after shopping at the grocery store, I drove home sobbing so hard, I started screaming in my car. I was terrified, but I didn't know why.

All that was to come—I think it came for me then. I turned, and with my turning, the shade of the lake changed. It was now a ringing, electric blue. The universe flattened against the sound.

~

July, its exits and entries. I've been trying to understand—or to attempt acknowledgement through inquiry, through exploratory articulation (Hejinian)—the nature of *opening* and *closing* (elevator doors). I need to say the phrase: tender approximations. I am, yes, aware of my own sentimentality around this process of inquiry through language. It's not separate from intensities of feeling. I move toward new formulations with a sense of renewal not distinct from my experience of bodily lusts and calms. It's language that craves and can also satiate. (Barthes: "I am interested in language because it wounds or seduces me.") A new movement in thinking immediately transforms my emotional reactivity around a recent desire.

Or a recent and total sense of loss. Grief, recovery, grief.

~

When the lightning starts, I'm its mirror. I know this by the way my eyes won't close. My body is reflective, immaterial, flashing. I can't sleep, can't scream, can't cry. Wait, I *can* cry. No, I can't (I stop abruptly). When the lightning flashes, I imagine a pair of traditional theater masks, drawn in neon lights in the sky.

Bolt, bolt, stillness.

Bolt. Bolt.

The window frame is a mirror frame. My chest is this sky, this storm; my chest is this square above the windowsill. In the bathroom I watch my eyes crinkle, my mouth grimace; then my face is expressionless; then I show my Cheshire teeth.

~

Everything I'm afraid of begins to happen. One day, you lie about something insignificant. You sleep with a new friend, a woman, and you tell me about it, but you become secretive. You say you're not thinking about her when you're with me, not texting with her, but you text her all week in my presence with your back to me.

You're moving faster, speaking faster; you're glittering. Glitter spurts from your eyes.

Then you say something significant, want to use a word you haven't used before. You're talking around it, so I say it for you, I say it first so that you can say it. *Gay.* Still, we make love for days before I drop you off at the bus station. You tell me you can feel gay and still feel attracted to me, that this is beautiful to you. But also, you say flatly, academically: "I guess we're giving up a certain kind of futurity, aren't we?"

You leave town for the weekend to be in the company of men. We decorate your face and your hair for them. You're going to stay with your new friend, the woman you slept with. She lives in another city, she wants to introduce you to some gay men who are her friends. Maybe you won't come back for me.

I stay inside my apartment with the curtains closed. I pace. Hours flood into each other, they slosh against the windows in the dark. Sentences flip into images, then flip back into words. The days and nights turn into each other, tricksters, shape-shifters. I can't find the exit, can't leave the circle we've drawn, the singular room, a lifetime of days.

"Time is the violent element that can make spatial configurations appear irrational," writes Hejinian. The brutal, slowed tick of the clock distorts the sites of our lovemaking: bedroom, body, mattress, memory. You're somewhere else, with someone else. I'm waiting for you to come back, even though you still won't be mine when you return. You call, but I don't want to talk to you on the phone, I can't. "I just need some time," I text. Your texts back: "My most beautiful, you my most beautiful."

By the time I pick you up four days later, you're nauseous with missing me. You say that you were wrong. It's around this time that two different Eliases mention Patti Smith's book *Just Kids* to me, which I won't read until later. Though it was recently that I read *Giovanni's Room*.

~

Hejinian: "Time sets the conditions for the surge of desire—whether erotic or epistemological—that…repeatedly casts the things of which it speaks (including desire itself) forward, into a distance in which they appear 'different' and then again 'different.'"

Ellaria pulled the young man's face to hers.

Oberyn: "Greedy."

"No?" she said to the young man.

"You're lovely. I just never acquired the taste."

I don't know now. Would you relate more to the young man in the scene? He's smooth, beautifully muscular, with something soft, submissive in the expression; youthful, sultry, with an unlined face; ready to be taken by the older man.

~

Patti Smith writes of her relationship with twentieth century photographer Robert Mapplethorpe: "In being open about his homosexuality, he feared our relationship would be destroyed. We needed time to figure out what all of this meant, how we were going to come to terms and redefine what our love was called."

~

"Over the weekend, I started feeling sick to my stomach thinking about losing you," you say. "I tried introducing myself as a gay man, and it didn't feel right. I missed you. I felt sick on the entire bus ride home."

~

Gerda, looking haggard, sitting on the ground against a wall in their apartment, when Einar comes home. "I thought you might not come back," Gerda says.

"That's absurd," Einar answers, though in the scene before, Lili meets up with a man in secret. And just before that, Eddie Redmayne (the cisgendered male actor who plays Einar/Lili) stands in front of a mirror, caressing his chest, then tucking his penis between his legs.

"Is it?" Gerda's eyes, humongous, dark, filled with something like shock or grief. Einar crouches beside her, gathers her into an embrace. Her body, limp; her eyes, unblinking.

Behind her is the portrait of Lili she'd feverishly drawn while alone in the apartment. In it, Lili sits sideways on a sofa, her arms crossed and draped over its back, her legs up on the cushions, bent at the knees. The viewer can see her pale back and her right side; her right breast is visible in profile. She's naked except for a pair of pointed gold oxfords with heels, and her auburn bob falls softly around her face, which is turned back over her shoulder. Her gaze is downward; she holds a cigarette. She looks alluring, coquettish, alive.

Gerda is distressed, but clearly also taken with Lili, moved by her.

~

We make love, achieving greater intensity each time than the time before. We're awake all night, we don't sleep at all—but in the morning, exhausted, I pass out for hours, while you're still awake, brimming with electricity. *Decreased need for sleep.* You barely eat. At night we're desperate to penetrate each other. We're each afraid we'll die.

Or that's what we want. "Kill me," I said once, beneath you. You said I was beautiful, that I was yours. You hit my face with your open palm again and again. "I love you so much. Kill me," I said. *Mine mine mine mine mine*, you whispered into my mouth, running your hands up and down my body while pushing into me. (I didn't want you to kill me—what did I mean?)

~

David, Baldwin's narrator in *Giovanni's Room,* writing about his fiancé: "I looked to Hella for help. I tried to bury each night, in her, all my guilt and terror. The need to act was like a fever in me, the only act possible was the act of love."

The pink glow of the streetlamp must be the same shade as before, but it seems darker, redder. The heat of summer is deafening.

When I touch you casually, you light up and grab me seriously. You seem frenetic, in love. But when I talk to you seriously, your expression is distracted, nonchalant, blithe. Your eyes look different. And your mouth—it's sometimes a different shape. Something else is wrong.

~

I leave town, I drive away alone. I'm at the point of breaking, fracturing, parts of me adrift, separating from other parts. Spaces in between.

Baldwin's David, again, about Hella: "I had never before clung to her as I clung to her during that time. But perhaps she sensed, from time to time, that my clutch was way too insistent to be trusted, certainly too insistent to last."

C, you were awake for days.

I was driving in the rain when I got a series of strange texts from you. An ordinary sentence, but you sent it one letter at a time. Then a full sentence, but you sent it over and over and over.

Later you described your full-blown mania to me: restlessness, high energy that vacillated from elation to agitation. You wanted to sing everything you said. You spoke incredibly fast, not always making sense. *Pressured speech.* Your thoughts moved so quickly, you couldn't distinguish between them and what you were saying aloud. *Subjective experience that thoughts are racing.*

You hit your head against a wall, hard, several times. You frightened the two women standing there in the office, your therapist and your psychiatrist.

I missed your first hospitalization.

~

What will the coming year bring?

The narrator will watch the violet blue ocean of her lover change to different kinds of emptiness, different kinds of accident.

When he's depressed, he'll get cold, he'll shiver so hard that his teeth chatter loudly. He'll move slowly, talk slowly. He'll lie down on her kitchen floor, say he wants to die. His mouth can hardly form the words. She'll drag him out for walks in the park, actually push his body along the path.

At the other end of the spectrum is heat, the pressing need for an outlet. When he starts crossing over into that fire, his body starts to shake uncontrollably. *Psychomotor agitation.* The night he finds out she slept with someone else, she'll watch him put out matches on his forearm, almost gleefully. She'll beg him to let her take him to the hospital. His eyes will be empty. He'll cut his ankle with a knife in the kitchen. A deep, fast cut; he'll bleed onto the hardwood floor of her apartment. "Did you see how easy that was?" he'll say, intrigued, impressed with himself. He won't want her to clean it up.

The lithium will make his hands tremble.

She'll drive him to the ER again and again. Sometimes she'll follow an officer's car there, because she won't like driving with him in the car when his movements are erratic. He'll slam his hand against the car window. He can go from silence to a sudden shout.

Or, once, the rapid naming of world rivers in a whisper. He won't remember this.

~

Meanwhile, something has clearly taken over her as well, not comparable to his condition, but linguistically linked.

Carson: "The lover mastered by eros cannot answer for his own mind or actions. From this condition, which the Greeks call erotic madness or *mania*, the lover's harmfulness ensues. As soon as eros enters his life, the lover is lost, for he goes mad. But where is the point of entry? When does desire begin? That is a very difficult moment to find, until it is too late."

The narrator thinks again of how her mother's life (and therefore her own) was determined by a secret that wasn't revealed until long after the death of its keeper. Perhaps what she's carried is not the desire for a secret, but the need to witness its destruction. Her point of entry was, after all, his revelation. But then more revelations came, one after another. A gap opened up, then another, then another, and she kept repeating the action of falling in.

~

It's early August when I come back from my road trip. We meet up at a café where once, early in our friendship, you admitted to me that you sometimes wanted to wear makeup.

At the time, I shrugged. But you panicked at having said it. You

54

looked around frantically, saw someone you worked with, and said, "Oh no, I know that guy."

I was confused. "It's okay," I said. Months later I would put peach eye shadow on you, paint your fingernails sea green. I would strap on a royal blue cock, call you my girl, take you.

Now I plan to tell you I can't see you anymore. I walk into the café, you're sitting at a table just inside the door. When our eyes meet we both start shaking. "Please," you say.

I'm in that café again. Your diagnosis was new; neither of us knew what to expect. I'm watching us that day, across from each other at the table, shaking, already touching, already agreeing to go back to my apartment.

~

Elias was a statue of a stag as he listened. We sat under a pavilion in the park. He was a statue of a man with his hand over his heart as he spoke. "This sounds like what all of literature is about. I feel very worried about you," he said. "Don't you want to write this kind of story, and not live it?" He embraced me, as a father might have, protectively, in a distant life.

~

Ellaria's blood-curdling scream chilled me. Her hands flew to her mouth, and her whole body shook, her eyes wide and wild, tear-filled, as the scream rang out. I felt nauseous, light-headed.

Oberyn was fighting The Mountain, a huge, ferocious hulk of a man, in one-on-one combat. And he was winning against this giant, but he got cocky, wanted to draw the death out, make it count. In a moment of thoughtlessness, Oberyn faced the arena's crowd theatrically. The Mountain, who was on his back on the ground, tripped him. The death was quick and horrific. The Mountain rolled over, and with his thumbs, he pressed Oberyn's eyes back into his skull, blood rushing from the two holes. Roaring, he crushed his skull; it exploded into a pool of blood.

Ellaria's scream seemed so much worse to me because of their last exchange: "Don't leave me alone in this world," she said as he entered the fighting arena, a note of genuine fear in her voice.

"Never," he promised.

(You and I discussed the parallels later: my love and fear for you; your one-on-one fight with your illness, your version of The Mountain. Also, the metaphor of your head exploding. We actually laughed.)

~

There are so many things to read on the internet. Late at night, unable to sleep beside one's sleeping lover, one might get up and read about vibrators, mood disorders, attachment theory, codependency, limerence, mixed-orientation marriages, hypersexuality, pharmaceutical drugs, success rates of the drugs, suicide rates for queers, women who want to rescue men, suicide rates for people with bipolar depression, electroconvulsive therapy, transfemininity, genderfluidity, family systems, ethical open relationships, genderqueer haircuts, polyamory, divorce rates, realistic dildos, harnesses, the emotional labor of women.

~

One morning, I told you I had a dream about Elias. You misheard me, at first thinking I'd said the name of your son. Your heart started pounding. You asked me to hide your medications.

I have dreamed of your wife, though I've never met her. The same dream, twice. We were all at a gathering with family and friends, and she and I were talking. It was pleasant. But later, I saw her asking people who I was.

~

Perhaps she'd been appearing in your dreams too.

This is how I feel when you leave me: our stillborn future, all the conversations we would have had, the conversations we are likely

57

having in another version of reality (imaginary paradise), suspended in the air, stagnant in your wake.

You'll step into the elevator, you'll leave me on a mezzanine. From that middle floor, that platform, I can see all the floors above and below where I stand.

We won't be able to look at each other when you come over to pick up your books.

~

The day before it happens, we sit with your friend Elias. We tell him we're in love, but that your diagnosis—now a month ago—has changed things. You crave the stability, the security of your prior existence: the house, the family. You wonder if treatment will change things for you, help you be monogamous, which is what that life requires. Your indiscretions, we now realize, were not only a symptom of repressed queerness—though they were this, too. But they were also due to the impulsivity and risk-taking behaviors associated with the disorder.

You need a place to rest. In your dreams, your son screams for you. You wake up sweating, crying, guilty. You're shaking with the other desire again, the one for your own blood.

"My love"—you, earlier that day, or later—"I'm crazy, I'm going to die, I'm going to kill myself, I'm afraid of it—"

One of us, both of us, fucking each other—later that evening, or earlier that morning—"I need you, without you I will explode, I will die, I need you, I'll never leave you, I want to share this life with you, take care of me, I'll take care of you, take care of me, I don't want to be in this world without you, I'll give you anything, I'll give you everything—"

You leave to go to therapy, and Elias and I talk about the benefits of you going back to your wife. I am extremely calm. "Your affect of objectivity," he says, shaking his head, "it's a thing to behold."

He isn't there to see it fall away.

~

The next day, the day it happens—you are haunted, the promise of your old life, your life *before*, feels more real to you with each hour—yes, I admit, I've been wishing to be rid of you, I've been fantasizing about escape, praying for it even, but when you leave me—

94

I simply want to be dead.
Weeping she left me

with many tears and said this:
Oh how badly things have turned out for us.
Sappho, I swear, against my will I leave you.

~

I fly to another city to visit friends (to disappear). A person named
Elias is living there. We met once years ago, when we were walking
diagonally in opposite directions through a plaza on a windy day.
In the center of that plaza, Elias dropped a red silk scarf, which I
saw and picked up. This object, this intermediary, this shred of color,
which was once theirs and is now mine, is the only contact we've
ever had. Perhaps this is why I won't recognize them at first when
I open the door.

I've been yanking up ice plant by the sea for hours when Elias sends
me a message asking if they can pick me up. I go downstairs, and
there they are in the street with their motorcycle. I reach out to shake
their hand, but instead we hug. "Here's your helmet," they say, and I
climb on behind them and slide my arms around their waist as we
ride through the old part of the city, bricks falling on us from the
buildings, which are burning.

Back at their place, they touch the bottoms of my feet. I don't flinch
at all.

"Elias, what do you do when your heart is broken, but you know it has to stay broken, you know you can't try to change or fix the situation, that you just have to let your heart be broken, maybe even continue to break?" I ask.

~

"It's difficult to give advice about a broken heart," says Elias. "It's hard, isn't it, to listen to advice when one's heart is broken. But what I want to say is this. Within every one of us is the energy of life, and that life has its own intelligence. As long as we're alive, its nature, I believe, is to heal and expand and go on living. And maybe the thing that stops us from seeing and feeling how close it is—extremely close, right under our skin—is the story that we create in our heads, moment to moment. A broken heart wields a very big story, one that we get attached to. But if you watch closely, it will ebb and flow. It's not the whole truth. In fact, the truth is far bigger."

"Thank you," I say, weeping—and seeing, finally, a path to letting go.

~

Except that when I return, I say to you, "Please." My body is a plea, it ignores every other kind of wisdom.

Anne Carson translates Sappho's fragment 94 as follows:

I simply want to be dead.
Weeping she left me

with many tears and said this:
Oh how badly things have turned out for us.
Sappho, I swear, against my will I leave you.   (In the next part of the fragment,
   Sappho attempts to be gracious)

And I answered her:
Rejoice, go and
remember me. For you know how we cherished you.   (But in the rest, perhaps she's trying
   to convince her lover to stay)

But if not, I want
to remind you

     ]and beautiful times we had.   (C, we had a beautiful spring and
   summer)

For many crowns of violets
and roses

     ]at my side you put on   (You donned my clothes)

and many woven garlands
made of flowers
around your soft throat.   (I mean don't leave me, I want to
   choke you again, I need to)

And with sweet oil
costly
you anointed yourself

(Get on your hands and
knees for me)

and on a soft bed
delicate
you would let loose your longing

(Your sweet moan, your back
arched, your tongue)

and neither any[   ]nor any
holy place nor
was there from which we were absent

no grove[   ]no dance
[no sound
[

~

Patti Smith, on one of her separations from Mapplethorpe (it took them many tries before they finally broke up for good): "Apart, we were able to see with even greater clarity that we didn't want to be without each other."

We're still under each other's spell. No distance between us will last.

Patti Smith: "Both of us had given ourselves to others. We vacillated…but we had found one another again."

"I love you more than breathing," you say.

At the end of summer, I ask you to come with me, and we leave together early, drive away from the city to a water cave on the sea. We get out of the car, strip in the afternoon light, dive into the waves, and pull ourselves into the cave along a stretch of tough wet rope. "Careful," I say. "The rocks are sharp. You'll want to lift your feet."

As we enter the cave, the water before us is black. Fragments of light enter through the small opening, shards of a mirror piercing the darkness, separating from the day. "Keep swimming forward," I say. Once we're all the way in, we turn around. The only light that illuminates the cave is coming up through the water, electric blue. It washes over our faces.

"Can I put my feet down now?" you ask.

"There's no bottom that we can touch," I say.

The water is bright blue and completely opaque, yet it has an odd, three-dimensional sheen. We can't see our bodies—as though they're gone.

~

When you start talking, I want to stop you, but instead I listen. Your words sting, even though my body doesn't exist. The fires of it stretch out and scatter, but not in the usual way. There's nothing here but paint, the blue surface of the water. Yet when you speak, there are also stairwells, the smell of herbs, Italian sunlight, the sound of chickens still awake in a yard in Mexico. Your words sting you too, wasps without bodies, tiny boxes of sharp sound. I touch one of the boxes, I try to look inside it, but the edge gets higher, or moves further away. You say more, and your words slap me in the face (erotic), your words sting my whole body, which doesn't exist, but which does exist, but which doesn't does doesn't beneath the blue leather, the water and light, light of the water, water of the night.

~

When I speak, the leather softens. We soften as though we are aging. The edges of our fantasies soften, the way an hour does. The skin of our hands and feet, creased like paper.

When I speak, my words sting you, and they sting me too.

I wonder if this stinging can turn into saying, if the saying can turn into being. The possibility brings splinters of relief, and I see them mirrored in your expression. I wonder if the stinging can be made to sing again, if it ever did sing, or whether or not it did. I wonder if the paper of our hands and feet, wrinkled from glowing for so long, can turn back into eucalyptus trees, where they belong. Your body belongs to another country, and I want to scream. The source isn't pleasure or pain, so I suppose it's "excess."

~

"If we're in here when the tide rises," I say, "the entrance to the cave will be covered with water. But we can still get out. We just have to hold our breath and swim through."

You look nervous. "I don't want to leave yet, but that sounds dangerous."

"Are you getting tired?" I ask.

You pause. "No," you say, but your eyes are glazed and half-shut.

~

Something is about to happen. I can tell because I hear a sound, or I almost do. I'm not sure if I hear it yet, but it's something like the anticipation of hearing, like when the musicians in the strings section of the orchestra lift their bows, and your ears perk up, expectant, simulating the sound of the first drawn-out note of a symphony you know well, one you love, have made love to many times.

I still don't know if I'm hearing anything or not, but now the sensation gets stronger. I think of Elias saying, "Many cats are out of the bag. At least three. Maybe there are more in there, who knows? What if you were like an eject button?"

"Maybe we should get out of here," I say, but my words are drowned out in a kind of crashing. It's either a large wave, or a spreading, crackling fire that breaks over us. It rips through the yard, burning the herbs. It spirals up the staircase to where I sit across from you in a plastic green chair under fluorescent lights during visiting hours. It stops before our faces, it looks us right in the face, it stares at us, it makes our faces gleam hotly, it glows the color of summer, stone fruit and roses, the color of streetlamps on a humid night, it hovers and trembles before us, it soaks us in its question, it's enamored with us, and we with it, we can barely move, we can't look away, it can't look away, we can't look away first, it can't.

~

I can tread water for hours. I wonder if I can do it for months, or years. I'm several feet away from you, but when you finally speak, I can feel the shape of the words in your mouth, as if my hands are the words, as if my hands are in your mouth. "It's too beautiful in here to leave," you say. I taste salt on your tongue.

I lay my head on a pillow. The cave flashes with fire, and in the electric blue flame, a sterile room without windows appears. There's only a thin hard bed. There are no objects with which you could harm yourself.

"Our bed is soft, made of silver blades of grass, turquoise waves, powder-white ash," I say.

"I'm afraid to go back through the cave's opening," you say. "It's hard for me to breathe."

You put your hand on your chest, and I feel it on mine. One of us gasps for air. My legs move continuously, swishing in the blue.

I see our figures, distant, in the oval mirror of autumn. Our image is the equinox, a door that must open. Across the threshold, in a different room, the ash leaves turn into red matches, already lighting and separating from the trees.

CB

for Kelly

ACKNOWLEDGMENTS & THANKS

Grateful thanks to Danielle Dutton and those who took her seminar, On Eros, in the fall of 2016 at Washington University in St. Louis. Special appreciation and thanks to Miranda Popkey for attentively reading and rereading versions of this work. Thank you also to the English Department at WashU; in particular, my boundless gratitude to Mary Jo Bang, Carl Phillips, Edward McPherson, and Kathleen Finneran.

Many people were present in my life while I was writing this work, in important ways that either directly or indirectly affected or supported the work: Sheila Munsey, Robin Munsey, Genevieve Munsey, Lauren and Jamie Stephens, Greg Heet, Niel Rosenthalis, Paige Webb, Stephanie Dering, James Scales, Jay Thompson, Melissa Dickey, Andy Stallings, Zach Savich, Laura Bylenok, Dan Beachy-Quick, Cole Swensen, Henri Cole, Amy Lee Ketchum, Andrea Lofthouse-Quesada, Christina Steurer, Gabe Boyer, Emma Slager, Ash Casteman, Courtney Casteman, Kate Benward, Cait Rippey, Hilary Plum, Jonathan McGregor, and Kelly Caldwell.

Immeasurable thanks to Zachary Doss, Brandi Wells, Vanessa Villarreal, Natalie Eilbert, and the rest of the team at Gold Line Press for bringing this chapbook into the world. Thank you to Todd Thomas Brown for the beautiful cover art. And thank you to Maggie Nelson, who saw something worthy in these words.

The following texts/films/shows are cited in this work: *Giovanni's Room* & *The Paris Review Interviews, II,* James Baldwin; *A Lover's Discourse* & *The Pleasure of the Text,* Roland Barthes; *Eros the Bittersweet,* Anne Carson; *The Danish Girl,* dir. Tom Hooper; *Game of Thrones,* created by David Benioff and D. B. Weiss; "Mock Orange," Louise Glück; "Regressive, Reductive and Harmful: A Trans Woman's Take On Tom Hooper's Embarrassing 'Danish Girl'," Carol Grant; *The Language of Inquiry,* Lyn Hejinian; "The Savage Mind," Claude Lévi-Strauss; *Handwriting* & *Running in the Family,* Michael Ondaatje; "Anyone Who Had a Heart," Carl Phillips; *If Not, Winter,* Sappho, trans. Anne Carson (see below); *Just Kids,* Patti Smith; *Transparent,* created by Jill Soloway; *Gravity and Grace,* Simone Weil, trans. Arthur Wills; *Sugar Break,* Maged Zaher.

"94 [I simply want to be dead.]" from IF NOT, WINTER: FRAGMENTS OF SAPPHO by Sappho, translated by Anne Carson, copyright © 2002 by Anne Carson. Used by permission of Alfred A. Knopf, an imprint of the Knopf Doubleday Publishing Group, a division of Penguin Random House LLC. All rights reserved. Any third party use of this material, outside of this publication, is prohibited. Interested parties must apply directly to Penguin Random House LLC for permission.

by William Youngblood

CASSIE DONISH is the author of the poetry collections *The Year of the Femme* (2019), winner of the Iowa Poetry Prize, and *Beautyberry* (2018). Her writing has appeared in *Best New Poets*, *The Cincinnati Review*, *Colorado Review*, *Gettysburg Review*, *jubilat*, *Kenyon Review Online*, *Tupelo Quarterly*, and elsewhere. She earned her MFA from Washington University in St. Louis, where she received an Olin Fellowship and served as the Junior Fellow in Poetry. She writes and works at the University of Missouri in Columbia.